Bill Caldwell

CARTOONS

DAILY STAR

Published by Annual Concepts Limited, One High Street, Princes Risborough, Buckinghamshire, HP27 0AG under licence from Express Newspapers plc. Printed in Italy. © 1992 Express Newspapers plc. ISBN 1-874507-03-1

£3.50

'It's nothing like L.A. Law.'

(Navratilova's lover claims millions in palimony case.)

September 13, 1991

'Hope you don't mind - I brought some Japanese friends home for dinner.'

(Charles visits London's Japanese festival.)

September 17, 1991

'It's only Selina Scott - she likes to avoid the cameras.'

September 19, 1991

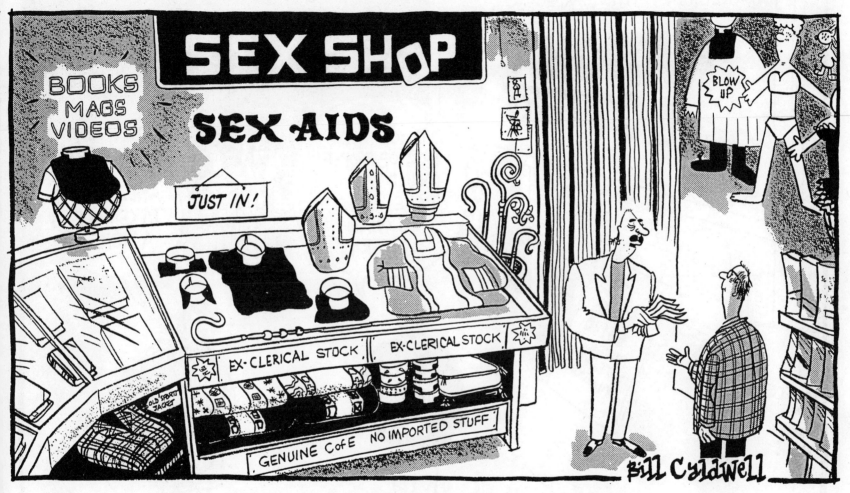

'Well, if you're sure you don't need this stuff any more, vicar.'

September 20, 1991

September 24, 1991

'They're either very very good or very very bad.'

(Football league clubs start playing on Sunday.)

September 27, 1991

'And here it is. . . the new dance craze they call DOIN' THE GAZZA.'

October 1, 1991

October 2, 1991

(Cigar advertising banned by the EC.)

October 3, 1991

'The usual, Miss Taylor?'

(Elizabeth Taylor marries for the eighth time.)

October 7, 1991

TORY CONFERENCE

BILL CALDWELL

'. . . And I can assure Mr Kinnock that we have the team to beat him when the time comes.'

(Western Samoa enjoys great success at Rugby World Cup.)

October 8, 1991

'I'm waiting for the Channel Tunnel link.'

October 10, 1991

'It was a friendly debate about the health service.'

October 11, 1991

'Doing anything after the sex harassment hearing, sugar?'

October 14, 1991

'And here we see the ancient ceremony of Changing the Staff at the Ministry of Defence.'

October 15, 1991

'OK. . . Just give us everything you own and nobody will get hurt.'

October 16, 1991

'And up. . . and lift. . . keep those tummies in. . . backs straight.'

TV-AM lose franchise.

October 17, 1991

'Quick, get undressed - you're on in two minutes.'

October 18, 1991

'Here's one I prepared earlier. . .'

October 22, 1991

'Psst! Can't you send it on microfilm like any other spy?'

(Daily Mirror executive named as Israeli spy.)

October 24, 1991

'Love the scenery, but where's all the wildlife?'

October 25, 1991

'A Dozen red Rovers? Your Lordship, you shouldn't have!'

October 30, 1991

'Thank God you're here, Doc - we thought we might miss the rugby.'

November 1, 1991

'He said he wanted to watch it all over again from the beginning. . .'

November 4, 1991

'We can't go yet — you missed one.'

November 5, 1991

'Never met him before - says he's acting for Ken Barlow.'

('Boring' Ken Barlow court case.)

November 6, 1991

'It's PARCEL-FORCE with the seeds you sent away for.'

November 7, 1991

'It's Ridley - Who let him out?'

November 11, 1991

'Sorry, gentlemen, Bum of the Year isn't the same thing. . .'

November 12, 1991

'Eddie the Eagle? I'm Victor the Vulture.'

November 13, 1991

'Well, he's looking better since I took away the Lucozade, doctor.'

November 14, 1991

'Honestly. . . No hard feelings, Mr Rushdie - you're entitled to slag off Britain if you wish!'

November 15, 1991

'Maggie's dang right, too - them Europeans are a weird bunch of critters.'

November 18, 1991

November 20, 1991

'Kamikaze strikers - we got them in a swap for Gary Lineker.'

November 21, 1991

'I'm sorry I must be off - I only go one round.'

November 22, 1991

'And what if we don't want to change our b****y money?'

November 27, 1991

'NEXT!'

November 28, 1991

'Not everybody gets an ex-Prime Minister-a-gram.'

November 29, 1991

December 2, 1991

COURTHOUSE

KENNEDY SMITH TRIAL EVIDENCE

EXHIBIT A

Bill Caldwell

'Well! You wouldn't catch me going on a date in stuff like that.'

December 4, 1991

'Are you SURE you didn't take it with you?'

December 5, 1991

'You SURE this is Maastricht?'

December 9, 1991

'Melvin? It's your mother. You didn't buy any of those BT shares, did you?'

December 10, 1991

'No more bread queues, mother—look what I found in the forest.'

December 11, 1991

(Maxwell case judge assaults cabby, mistaking him for a journalist.)

December 12, 1991

'It's the man from the building society - we've fallen behind with our payments.'

December 13, 1991

'Doing anything tonight, Moneypenny?'

December 18, 1991

'There's a Halifax mortgage, or you can rent if the payments get too much.'

December 19, 1991

'Nintendo? Sure thing, sonny.'

December 20, 1991

'Brace yourself, mother - it's another one of Andrews ***** jokes.'

December 23, 1991

'Well? What wonderful bargains did you get in the sales, dearest?'

December 27, 1991

January 6, 1992

'It's good news - the British beef was OK.'

(British meat sent to relieve starvation in Russia held up by tests for mad cow disease.)

January 7, 1992

'Why, Miss Parton! I didn't recognise you without your . . . er . . . implants.'

January 8, 1992

'Anything you say may be taken down by somebody who can read and write.'

(Police introduce very very easy spelling tests for new recruits.)

January 10, 1992

'Your secret's out, Albert - there was no one-night stand in 1945.'

January 13, 1992

January 14, 1992

'My lawyer instructs me I need say nothing regarding the whereabouts of your housekeeping.'

January 15, 1992

'It'll never come out.'

(Private photos of Fergie and Steve Wyatt start furore.)

January 16, 1992

'It's the Duchess of York - she has to be careful who she's seen with.'

January 17, 1992

January 20, 1992

'And there's going to be a Kinnock tax on luxury cardboard boxes.'

January 21, 1992

'OK. We're saving money on the band but what's it going to cost in batteries?'

(Big cut back in army band costs.)

January 23, 1992

'Ahem! This isn't a library, you know.'

(New magazine specialising on tips for saving money goes on sale in USA.)

January 24, 1992

'But you can't just say: Stuff the election!'

(John Major is guest on Desert Island Discs.)

January 27, 1992

'What did I tell you about smoking in front of the Minister, darling?'

January 28, 1992

'Hell. . . who wants to be President anyway?'

(Senator Bill Clinton's race for the Whitehouse threatened by sex scandal.)

January 29, 1992

'Well . . . when the President said 'Let's get these missiles outa here'!'

January 30, 1992

February 3, 1992

'WELL I'M SORRY PHILIP, BUT IT'S ALL WE CAN AFFORD.'

February 4, 1992

'Sweet and sour monkey . . . monkey with bamboo shoots . . . monkey fried rice.'

February 5, 1992

'You're supposed to just ask them if they plan to vote for you, Mr Ashdown.'

February 6, 1992

'Of course, the monarchy's changed quite a bit over the years.'

February 7, 1992

'I'm sure it was left, left again, **then** right.'

February 10, 1991

'When do the Chippendales come on?'

February 11, 1992

'You quite sure you heard Princess Diana was visiting the Taj Mahal?'

February 12, 1992

'Well . . . if HE says we're still in it, we're still in it.'

February 13, 1992

(After Paddy Ashdown's affair leaked to the press, other MP's afraid of similar exposure.)

February 14, 1992

'OK, you can put Mr Jagger's Zimmer frame back together — he's clean.'

February 18, 1992

'Look Salman, when I said what form of protection do you use . . .'

February 20, 1992

'Typical! It's lunchtime, only one till open and we're stuck behind Sara Keays.'

February 21, 1992

'By heck, luv — a jogging lamplighter.'

March 4, 1992

'. . . and so BR Passenger's Charter, chapter 81, page 369, clause 14c clearly states . . .'

March 5, 1992

'And when Mr Botham enters he'd like us to curtsey thus . . .'

March 6, 1992

'No, you can't pay me after you get some tax back.'

March 9, 1992

'Yes, Norman . . . very subtle!'

March 10, 1992

'We'll take two.'

March 12, 1992

'It was getting a bit much really - this bloke coming round every five years. . .'

March 13, 1992

'Thank God your food has lasted out - we're starving.'

(Last Soviet cosmonaut, Sergie Krikalev, rescued after year in space to return to newly formed C.I.S.)

March 17, 1992

'Go straight in — they're expecting you.'

March 18, 1992

(Labour and Tory parties release their manifestos.)   March 19, 1992

'Whatever next?'

March 20, 1992

'I got that for playing the part of a duchess.'

March 23, 1992

'He's slept right through it — any volunteers to wake him?'

March 25, 1992

'He didn't go for a duck - it was some Aussie impersonator.'

March 26, 1992

'Well . . . have you heard of a charity group called Trading Places?'

March 27, 1992

'. . . And I'd like to thank my plastic surgeon . . . my implant surgeon . . .'

March 31, 1992

'April fool!'

April 1, 1992

'He's a striker all right but he can't get it in the box.'

April 3. 1992

April 9, 1992

'Still looks like a hung Parliament, then?'

April 10, 1992

Bill Caldwell

'Cheer up, Mr Kinnock — at least it's a job.'

April 13, 1992

'Hurry Luigi! Your a spaghetti's a getting hot.'

April 14, 1992

'Good news, Your Highness?'

April 15, 1992

'You quite sure he's the £2 million pools winner?'

(£2 million pools winner keeps identity secret.)

April 16, 1992

'Ooh . . . You must be . . . Oooh . . . don't tell me . . .'

April 21, 1992

'It's how he would have wanted it.'

April 22, 1992

'Legalise brothels? Do you want to take the fun out of it?'

April 23, 1992

'Don't just lie there - make the Earth move AGAIN.'

April 24, 1992

'I preferred Order, Order.'

April 28, 1992

'I don't like this movie.'

May 1, 1992

'The bed's too wide.'

May 5, 1992

'Come on, Jimmy - aren't you being a bit hasty?'

(Jimmie White loses yet another World snooker championship.)

May 6, 1992

♪ 'Underneath the lamplight, by the Pearly Gates . . .' ♪

May 7, 1992

'God, it's Souness — who sold his ticket?'

(Souness, ill in hospital, not expected to turn up at Cup Final.)

May 8, 1992

'That reminds me — I wonder how Charles is?'

May 12, 1992

(3 US astronaut's dramatic spacewalk to manually realign satellite.)

May 15, 1992

'Evening, Mr Mansell - the usual?'

May 19, 1992

'Can't you watch it on BSkyB like everyone else?'

May 20, 1992

'Not much wrong with this environment.'

June 2, 1991

'At least there's a guaranteed sunbed.'

(German company buys Thomas Cook.)

June 5, 1992

'Well SOMEONE'S still talking.'

(Search continues for royal marriage palace informer.)

June 9, 1992

'No .. really .. there's no need to kneel.'

June 10, 1992

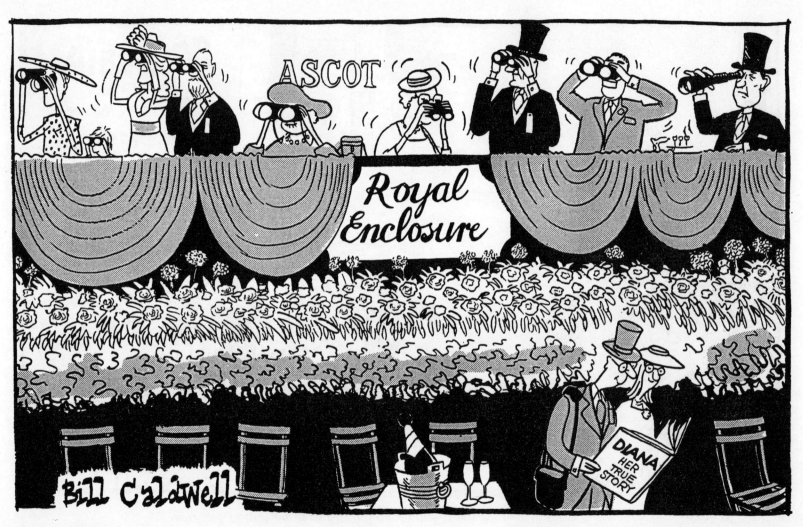

Bill Caldwell

June 17, 1992

'Now then, Sunshine — I expect you're wondering why we pulled you over.'

(For first time Home Secretary withdraws a Police Authority's Certificate of Efficiency.)

June 24, 1992

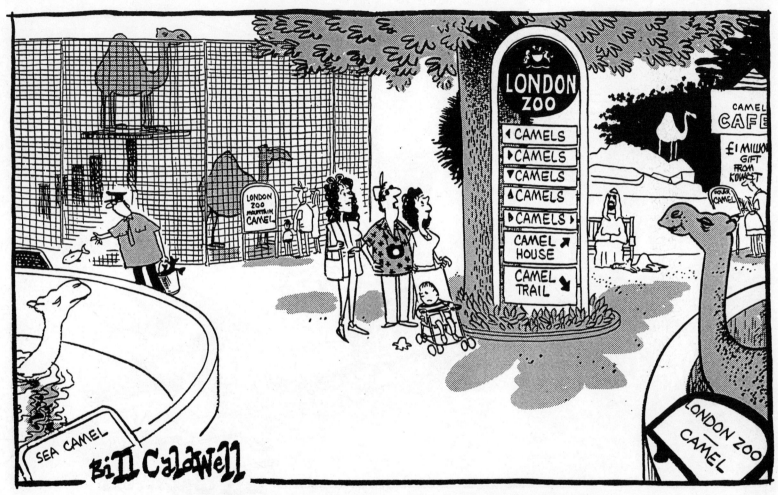

'The Emir of Kuwait's been a big help in keeping this place open.'

June 25, 1992